DSC SPEED READS
PERSONAL DEVELOPMENT

Confidence at Work

Chrissie Wright

directory of social change

Published by the Directory of Social Change (Registered Charity no. 800517 in England and Wales)

Office: Suite 103, 1 Old Hall Street, Liverpool L3 9HG

Tel: 020 4526 5995

Visit www.dsc.org.uk to find out more about our books, subscription funding website and training events. You can also sign up for e-newsletters so that you're always the first to hear about what's new.

The publisher welcomes suggestions and comments that will help to inform and improve future versions of this and all of our titles. Please give us your feedback by emailing publications@dsc.org.uk.

It should be understood that this publication is intended for guidance only and is not a substitute for professional advice. No responsibility for loss occasioned as a result of any person acting or refraining from acting can be accepted by the author or publisher.

Print and digital editions first published 2022

Copyright © Directory of Social Change 2022

All rights reserved. No part of the printed version of this book may be stored in a retrieval system or reproduced in any form whatsoever without prior permission in writing from the publisher. This book is sold subject to the condition that it shall not, by way of trade or otherwise, be lent, re-sold, hired out or otherwise circulated without the publisher's prior permission in any form of binding or cover other than that in which it is published, and without a similar condition including this condition being imposed on the subsequent purchaser.

The digital version of this publication may only be stored in a retrieval system for personal use. No part may be edited, amended, extracted or reproduced in any form whatsoever. It may not be distributed or made available to others without prior permission in writing from the publisher.

The publisher and author have made every effort to contact copyright holders. If anyone believes that their copyright material has not been correctly acknowledged, please contact the publisher, who will be pleased to rectify the omission.

The moral right of the author has been asserted in accordance with the Copyrights, Designs and Patents Act 1988.

ISBN 978 1 906294 08 3 (print edition)
ISBN 978 1 78482 100 5 (digital edition)

British Library Cataloguing in Publication Data
A catalogue record for this book is available from the British Library

Cover and text design by Kate Griffith
Printed and bound in the UK by Martins the Printers, Berwick upon Tweed

Contents

Introduction		**4**
Chapter 1:	**Confidence, self-esteem and values**	**5**
	▪ What is confidence?	5
	▪ How confident are you?	6
	▪ How is self-esteem related to confidence?	6
	▪ Your personal values	7
	▪ From values to goals	8
Chapter 2:	**Emotional intelligence**	**10**
	▪ Emotional intelligence and confidence	10
	▪ Changing your thinking to manage your feelings	11
Chapter 3:	**Building assertiveness**	**14**
	▪ Communication behaviours	14
	▪ What is assertive behaviour?	15
	▪ Assertive behaviours at work	15
Chapter 4:	**Looking the part**	**24**
	▪ Looking and sounding confident	24
	▪ Building credibility	27
Chapter 5:	**If things go wrong**	**29**
	▪ Developing resilience	30
	▪ Your well-being is important	31
	▪ Final word	32

Introduction

Who will this book help?

This book is for anyone who needs a confidence boost at any time. You may be starting out in your working life, navigating your way around a new role or organisation, or returning to work after a lengthy absence. You could be facing a fresh challenge or picking yourself up after a perceived failure or setback. Equally, you may simply need to refresh your sense of your self-worth. The workplace can be daunting at times, and no matter what your position is in your organisation, this book will help you to move forward with courage and confidence.

What will it give you?

This book will help you to understand the differences between the inter-related qualities of confidence, self-esteem and assertiveness and how you can build each of them up by setting a firm foundation of personal values and goals.

It includes practical techniques you can use in a variety of common work situations to communicate positively and with confidence. There are tools for communicating assertively and dealing with feedback.

If you need a bit of extra help handling the knock-backs of the workplace and strengthen your self-assurance in life too, this book will be your guide.

Chapter 1

Confidence, self-esteem and values

This chapter looks at what confidence is and how it relates to self-esteem and personal values.

What is confidence?

Those of us who are not confident stand open-mouthed with wonder at people who seem to march through life without a single care in the world. We experience confidence, as well as lack of it, as a powerful feeling or emotion, which then reflects in how we hold ourselves. When things go well and we feel good about ourselves, we can exude a compelling sense of assuredness and positivity – the very characteristics of confidence. On the other hand, when things do not work out, we can feel anxious, negative and withdrawn, and our whole being displays that message. Some of us can feel a lack of confidence even when things *are* going well – unconfident people tend to think that success is luck and failure is their fault. The confidence challenge is, in part, about learning to appear confident even when 'curling up' inside. Former British Prime Minister Harold Macmillan reputedly claimed there was never a time when he had to speak in public that he did not feel absolutely sick inside (nobody could see that, though!).

There is not a straightforward definition of confidence. Dictionary definitions tend to define confidence in terms of trusting and being able to rely on something or someone. This reminds us that we need to learn to trust and rely on ourselves as well as other people. Trusting yourself to 'have a go' does not guarantee a positive outcome, but not feeling sure of yourself and trying anyway is a sure way to build confidence.

Confidence ebbs and flows in different areas and times of our lives. It comes as we learn new things about ourselves and the world around us. The good news is that confidence can be developed at any stage.

How confident are you?

What is your assessment of your confidence levels right now? As a starting point, think about the following questions:

- What would confidence look and feel like to me?
- What are the areas in my life that I feel confident about now?
- What do I like about myself?
- What positive feedback have I received?
- What stops me from focusing on positive rather than negative comments towards me?
- In which area of my work (or broader – life) would I most like to develop confidence?

> **Top tip**
> Keep a journal of all positive feedback you receive – both in and outside work. We tend to remember our 'failures' and forget our many successes – great and small.

How is self-esteem related to confidence?

Although related, confidence and self-esteem are not the same. Self-esteem is about self-appraisal and forms the foundation through which we think, feel, act and determine our relationship to ourselves, others and the world.

Self-esteem refers to your overall opinion of yourself. Having high self-esteem means you value yourself more, understand your strengths and believe in yourself to achieve new goals. In contrast, low self-esteem can make you lack confidence and feel incompetent and inadequate. Over time, these negative feelings can cause you to undervalue yourself and frustrate your ability to step up to opportunities.

> **Where next?**
> See the Rosenburg Self-Esteem Scale:
>
> *https://openpsychometrics.org/tests/RSE.php*

It may seem that confidence stems from self-esteem; however, it is more of a virtuous circle: building self-esteem enhances your outer and inner confidence, and the confidence to take on new challenges improves your self-esteem. Both confidence and self-esteem are programmed through early experiences in life, but that does not mean you cannot work on managing and improving them.

Your personal values

> **Top tip**
> Values are relatively stable, but as you go through life and your view of success changes, you will need to revisit and redefine them.

You can start building a foundation for confidence and self-esteem by establishing what matters to you and brings a sense of stability and safety: your own personal values.

You may not always be aware of the values that exist in your sub-consciousness until you actually dig deep and name them. To help recognise and understand your values, a good starting point may be to think about different roles you play in your life, such as employee, manager, volunteer, sibling, friend, carer, neighbour and so on. Then, thinking about each of these roles, ask yourself 'What do I value most?' The table on the next page shows an example of what values might be associated with different roles.

Role	Values
Employee	Money, creativity, freedom
Manager	Work, responsibility, learning
Carer	Responsibility, family, strength
Friend	Honesty, support, loyalty
Neighbour	Safety, kindness, security

Having set out everything that you value in relation to your roles in work and life, identify and prioritise your top three overall values to frame your personal statement of values, as in the example below.

Personal statement of values
1. Family is most important to me
2. Climate change is the key external concern for me
3. Mutual respect in all interactions is not negotiable

From values to goals

Establishing your personal values can give you more certainty and direction to frame your specific goals. Building confidence and self-esteem is a great deal easier when you have a clear idea of what it is you want to achieve. To move from values to goals, ask yourself:

- What is important to me in my work and life?
- When and where do I feel my skills and abilities are applied best?
- How does my work fit into my current lifestyle and circumstances?
- Do I have a career plan and what would career success look like to me?
- What are the things I feel most passionate about or know I can do well?
- What kind of environment and organisational culture do I work well in?

The mind is a goal-achieving mechanism, and all achievements – large or small – that help you realise your aims and values enhance self-esteem and the feeling of self-efficacy.

Understanding yourself through your personal values and goals also enables you to manage your feelings more effectively. Sometimes, you may feel uncomfortable or upset without really knowing why and that can affect your confidence. Often, these feelings surface because something is compromising your values or impeding your goals. Self-management of your emotional state is a key competency of emotional intelligence, the subject of the next chapter.

Why work–life balance matters

Life is not just about work. The values you have and the goals you set will relate to your wider life as well. It is important to look at the bigger picture: what other areas of your life are important to you? If you feel forced to make sacrifices in certain areas of your life, you may feel unhappy and uncomfortable because you are, albeit subconsciously, violating your values. Consider the following areas of life in terms of how important they are to you and how much attention you are currently dedicating to them:

Area of life	Importance to me (1–10)	Attention given (1–10)
Time spent with family		
My social life and time spent with friends		
Personal development/intellectual		
Leisure activities, hobbies and interests		
Contributing to my community		
Taking good physical care of myself		
(Add your own example relevant to you)		

Note the biggest gaps in scores between what is important to you and how much attention you are dedicating to it. This will help you identify areas to work on. See page 31 for more on how to keep a healthy work–life balance and look after your well-being.

Chapter 2

Emotional intelligence

This chapter looks at how emotional intelligence helps build a confident mindset.

Emotional intelligence and confidence

We are emotional creatures, but we may not always be aware that our emotions influence our thinking and behaviour and impact on our ability to feel confident. Emotions are a survival mechanism necessary to help and protect us, particularly when responding to a new situation or a perceived threat. In stressful circumstances, our bodies can go into 'fight or flight' mode, designed to help us deal with the situation: our thinking brain stops working and we are on high alert ready to fight, flee or freeze. However, you might feel overwhelmed by fear and distress, and experience a strong physical reaction (known as 'emotional hijack'), which manifests through things like a faster heartrate, a churning stomach and the inability to think clearly. Feeling or even looking confident can become challenging in such circumstances. It is, however, possible to manage those feelings of anxiety if you remind yourself that it is your brain preparing you for unfamiliar territory and that it is OK to feel nervous. This understanding is at the heart of emotional intelligence.

Emotional intelligence boils down to your ability to express emotions appropriately and clearly in a way that enables you to achieve harmonious and effective outcomes for yourself and others. There are two domains of emotional intelligence, which can be defined as:

1. **Intrapersonal skills**: your relationship with yourself in understanding and recognising your feelings, managing them and motivating yourself.

2. **Interpersonal skills**: your relationships with other people through recognising their emotions and handling social interactions.

Self-confidence is one of the key competencies of emotional intelligence, because recognising and managing your emotions can help you feel more self-assured. If you are able to manage your feelings, it is easier to pick yourself up after setbacks and adjust to the changing environment and challenges. Similarly, being able to recognise other people's emotions puts you on a surer footing when engaging with them.

Changing your thinking to manage your feelings

Our mind and body are closely linked. Although the 'fight or flight' mechanism is there to protect us, it does not always serve us in our current world. At work, a thought about something stressful (e.g. a deadline or meeting) or our boss asking to see us may trigger a strong reaction and inhibit our thinking.

Being your inner coach

The good news is that you can change how you feel by being your own inner coach and reframing your thoughts to prevent your mind from going into a spiral of self-defeating imaginings. Reframing is changing how we see something and then expressing it differently. It sounds easy enough but is not always so, because our emotions dominate our responses before our rational-thinking brain has time to catch up. (There is truth in the saying 'take a deep breath and count to ten'.)

Reframing your thinking

Is your glass half empty or half full? We tend to be one or the other when facing new challenges, which is the best time to build your confidence and work on reframing your thinking. Try these practical techniques:

- Challenge your internal critic:

Internal critic might say	Reframe with new thinking
'I can't stand it! I can't do it!'	'If it does not work out, I can do something to fix it.'
'This always happens. It's not fair.'	'This has happened before, but I can try something different to break the cycle.'
'Why am I so stupid!'	'I know how valuable I am.'
'There's too much to do.'	'I'm not afraid of tackling the tough stuff first, and then I can do all the easy things.'
'This is not my job. I shouldn't have to do this.'	'I always have choices.'
'I feel terrible.'	'I am going to take good care of myself.'

- Be aware of the language you use in your thinking: even single words can make us feel defeated and depressed. Words like 'have to', 'should' or 'must' can feel like you are carrying heavy boulders on your shoulders. Instead, try reframing to: 'can', 'will', 'choose to' and 'want to' to feel lighter and more motivated. For example, instead of saying 'I must do this difficult report on a subject I don't properly understand', frame it as 'I choose to try new things and learn about a challenging topic'.

- Remind yourself that thoughts are not 'the truth' or 'reality' – they are just a bunch of ideas that we create about our lives. Recognise that any ideas about the future are speculative and may never actually happen, and any thoughts about the past or present are just one of many possible perceptions.

- Give yourself time and space to slow down, take a little bit of time out and consider all options. When you are in 'fight or flight' mode, it is easy to react instinctively (or hard not to when overwhelmed by emotion). Taking a deep breath and counting to ten allows your thinking brain to kick in. The danger is that by reacting impulsively you may deny yourself an opportunity that could really help you grow and increase your confidence.

- Avoid exaggerating and catastrophising – how bad is the situation really? Ask yourself 'What are the *facts* about the situation and what are my *feelings*?' Emotions can easily distort reality to the point where we make a mountain out of a molehill. Imagine yourself looking at the situation from the outside in, or that you are someone else sizing up the facts of the situation.

- Try not to over-generalise. One failure or mistake is not the slippery slope to disaster. Learn from it and try again. An error that causes a delay in your project does not mean that the project is doomed or that you can't do anything on time. Failure is only feedback.

- Always look for the positives, even if the situation just seems so bad that, at first, there are no obvious ways forward. After something has happened and we are looking back at the situation, we are often able to note some good things, even if it is only the fact that we survived.

- Looking at the long-term scenario can help. Remind yourself of the longer-term benefits – your ultimate goal – and see tackling a short-term issue as a pathway to further opportunities.

Chapter 3
Building assertiveness

This chapter looks at types of communication behaviour and assertiveness in the workplace.

Communication behaviours

An assertive person can appear confident even if they are wobbling inside. Assertive behaviour can be learned, but it is important to distinguish it from three other types of behaviour:

- **Passive behaviour**: is the failure to stand up for yourself and your rights effectively. The intention may be self-protection in terms of being safe and letting others take responsibility for you.
- **Aggressive behaviour**: violates the rights of others. It is often dominating, attacking, accusatory and judgemental. The intention is to be on top – 'I am OK, you are not'.
- **Passive-aggressive behaviour**: occurs where a person appears passive on the surface but are really acting out anger in a subtle, indirect way. The intention behind such behaviour may be driven by the need to control and manipulate those around to avoid confrontation and the risk of rejection.

What is assertive behaviour?

All communication behaviours are choices that are made in any given situation, but the more assertive you are, the more your confidence and self-esteem will grow. Assertive behaviour promotes fairness in human interactions and is based on respect for yourself and others. It means feeling in control of yourself and being able to express your needs, wants and opinions without feeling overly fearful and without punishing, threatening or putting down another person. It includes:

Where next?
Assess your assertiveness with this questionnaire:

www.nswnma.asn.au/wp-content/uploads/2020/05/How-Assertive-are-You-Questionaire-FS.pdf

- **Expressing positive feelings:** showing appreciation, receiving and accepting compliments, asking for help, making requests and assuming you will be taken seriously.
- **Expressing negative feelings:** such as communicating hurt, appropriately and respectfully notifying annoyance and making complaints.
- **Standing up for your legitimate rights:** such as setting boundaries (saying no), expressing personal opinions, refusing to be put down and taking ownership of an action or a situation.
- **Communicating clearly**: saying what you think calmly and decisively, and firmly advocating your rights and needs without violating those of others.

Being assertive means understanding that your rights are just as valid and important as anyone else's including:

- The right to make mistakes. This means that you have the responsibility to own your mistakes and not blame others for them.
- The right to judge your own behaviour, thoughts and emotions. Also, the obligation to take responsibility for your behaviour.
- The right to say 'no' and 'I don't know'.

Assertive behaviours at work

It is not always straightforward to learn new behaviours and to take on board different approaches that may initially feel very alien. Being able to distinguish assertive behaviours from the other three types of communication behaviour (see page 14) is the first step. You then need to try acting assertively often enough so that such behaviour becomes embedded and starts building confidence and self-esteem. Practise assertive behaviours by applying the tips for key working life situations covered in the following sections.

Saying 'no' to your boss or colleague

Setting boundaries is an important aspect to being assertive. Being clear about your rights and values will help you know when you have a legitimate right to refuse a request. Imagine being asked to work late without prior warning when you already have an important appointment you do not want to miss. Firstly, remember that the person asking has the right to do so, but you, in turn, have the right to refuse. Saying 'no' is tough, especially when it is to your boss, whom you want to please and accommodate. Acknowledge the request and, if possible, give your reason for refusing it. Be concise and polite but do not make profuse apologies. Remember:

- Be aware of using a firm steady voice and maintain eye contact.
- Be prepared to offer/discuss an alternative ('I can work late tomorrow').
- If the other party persists, say 'no' with firmness and repeat without justifying or explaining further: 'No, I'm sorry I can't.'

One-to-ones with your manager

The relationship with your manager is important for your development. It takes time to build a relationship of trust and mutual understanding and one-to-one meetings are an opportunity for this. An assertive approach means being honest and open, while appreciating the role and perspective of your manager:

- Do not postpone or avoid meetings – regular catch-ups help build relationships.

- Listen to understand and ask questions for clarification.
- Do not just accept everything that you are told or be afraid to raise issues that may be worrying or concerning you. Use assertive language by owning your feelings, for example: 'I feel uncomfortable when you criticise me in front of other team members, which is what happened at last week's team meeting.' This way, you are focusing on the behaviour rather than the person concerned.
- Remember you have rights as an employee: the right to know what your job is, who your boss is and what is expected of you.
- Work on understanding your manager's style of communication and try to meet them halfway.
- If you receive critical feedback, try not to react emotionally but listen and ask questions to establish the facts. Remember that feedback is not necessarily the truth – it may be opinion, and you have the power to choose whether to take it on board. Sometimes, though, the harshest feedback is what takes you forward and, in the long run, helps you the most.
- Test out your aspirations for your future with your manager. Show that you are keen to take opportunities for new learning and development.
- Ensure you follow up any agreed actions and reviews going forward.

One-to-ones with your staff and colleagues

When you are the manager, one-to-ones with staff are a key component of performance management. As a manager, you may sometimes have to have difficult conversations and give critical feedback, so clarity and confidence in such situations is important. Equally, one-to-ones with colleagues are vital in building successful relationships, so you should treat them with importance and allocate an appropriate amount of time for these meetings.

- Allow enough time for one-to-ones. Give your full attention and shut out noise and distractions. Listen with empathy and keep an open mind.
- Prepare for the meeting – catch up on previous notes and prepare a shared agenda, so that the conversation has structure and purpose.

- When giving difficult feedback, remain calm, kind and constructive. Ensure that the conversation is positively framed: explain the constructive purpose of the feedback. Agree a positive action and outcomes going forward.
- In all conversations, listen actively and do not get side-tracked. Do not dominate the conversation and try to engage the other person.
- When giving factual feedback, be clear and precise. Try to maintain a relaxed facial expression and body language.
- Be clear about timelines for any actions and follow up going forward.

Social situations at work

Social situations can be daunting for people who may be naturally introverted or those who may suffer from social anxiety in larger groups. However, learning to navigate social situations at work is a good opportunity to practise confidence and, over time, feel more comfortable:

- Rather than avoiding social situations, try putting yourself in a variety of them and challenge yourself to start conversations with others. Have in mind conversation openers – introducing yourself and asking questions.
- Listen actively: show interest in others, which will make them feel valued and heard, and focus on what the other person is saying to enable you to reply with a thoughtful response to keep the conversation going.
- If you do not feel socially confident, it can be tempting to look for evidence to confirm your belief. Do not assume that others' reactions are caused by you. Realise that others' responses are a product of those people and not you. For example, if someone ended a conversation with you quickly and ran off, ask yourself if it could be due to other things and not you. Maybe the person was unwell or late, or they lacked confidence themselves.
- Be aware of your body language: smile to show interest and that you are relaxed (even if you are not). Make eye contact to show others that you are listening to them. Avoid fidgeting or swaying so you do not look nervous.

- Speak clearly and at a level so that others can hear you. Mumbling is hard to hear and suggests that you do not want to be heard. Do not speak too quickly, and if you speed up, take a pause before continuing.
- If the person you are trying to speak to is not responding, that is not on you. Be tough, shrug it off and move on to the next person.
- Avoid getting stuck with one person who is very happy to talk at you. Try using their name to interrupt them – we always tend to pause at the sound of our own name – and say that you need to catch someone before they leave or that you have promised to speak to another person.

Working with intimidating colleagues

Intimidating colleagues can make your days at work uncomfortable and difficult. They do not have any real power over you, like the authority your boss has, but they have perceived power, which can still feel threatening. Aim to overcome this feeling and ensure that you are not pushed into doing anything against your will.

- Practise and rehearse assertive responses at home with 'I' statements, like 'I think... ' or 'I feel...'. Never use aggressive language or phrases like 'You never...' or 'You always...'. These statements trigger other people and tend to make them defensive. By using 'I' language, you are owning your feelings and dealing with the behaviour, not the person.
- Think of responses you can use to rebuff behaviour, but remember you can take your time. You do not have to give an instant answer. Force yourself to appear calm and unruffled – even if you are momentarily intimidated.
- Do not allow the intimidator to trigger an aggressive response. Apply the 'fogging' technique if you can. This means putting a mental space between yourself and the intimidator, and rebutting their comments and accusations by saying things like 'You're not really serious, are you?' and 'Don't rush me – I am considering what you've said', or taking any criticisms on board without defending them as in 'Well yes, I haven't answered your question'. 'Fogging' is like wrapping yourself in metaphorical cotton wool.

- Break the cycle of feeling belittled or pushed aside by concentrating on your desired outcome. You can be firm without sounding aggressive or angry.
- Ask yourself 'What am I really afraid of? How can these colleagues really hurt me?' Resolve to stand up to them while remaining professional.

Speaking up at meetings

Meetings can be daunting, especially if you are not used to attending and participating in them. Whether face-to-face or online, it is common to feel anxious and self-conscious in a meeting. You might worry you will be ignored or shot down by louder voices, but meetings are an opportunity to be noticed and show that you can be assertive in a positive way that contributes to the successful outcomes for the group.

- Prepare for the meeting. Study the proposed agenda and any accompanying information.
- Understand why you have been invited to the meeting; it is likely that you have relevant knowledge, skills or information – so you have reason to be confident! Alternatively, your manager might think it is a good learning opportunity for you, so view the meeting as a chance to develop.
- Try to ensure you speak within the first 15–20 minutes of the meeting. If you are heard early, it is easier to speak up subsequently.
- Ask questions. If putting your own view across is too nerve-racking at first, begin by asking questions about what others are saying. But do not overdo this, as asking too many questions can delay the meeting.
- You can also build confidence by supporting and speaking up for others by saying you agree with what someone has said or by asking someone who has been interrupted ('Alex, what were you going to say?'). Soon you will start to feel more confident about speaking up for yourself.
- Be aware of your body language – even when you are just sitting and listening at the meeting. Maintaining eye contact with the person speaking and nodding in agreement shows that you are alert and respectful.
- Get yourself on the agenda to have a guaranteed opportunity to speak.

- Speak clearly and concisely, having prepared in advance if possible. Start and end with conviction and avoid opening with an apology ('I'm sorry, but...').
- Avoid, if you can, saying 'I disagree' – people hear this and feel confronted and may stop listening. Try instead 'I see this a little differently'.
- Remain positive and constructive – challenge ideas instead of people and be respectful of everyone at the meeting at all times.

Public speaking and giving presentations

In surveys of human fears, public speaking is regularly cited as one of the poll toppers. So, you are not unusual or alone if you feel a dramatic loss of confidence when faced with this situation. Take a pro-active approach:

- Allow yourself enough preparation time. Research your audience beforehand, work on a clear, simple structure, and practise your timings and your speech in front of the mirror. Use cue cards you can read at a glance. Do not read out word for word unless you are giving a formal lecture.
- Be your positive inner coach: imagine yourself doing this really well. Think back to times when you have done well in this context.
- It is OK to admit if you do not know something. Be honest – audiences respect that. If you forget something, just tell your audience what is happening. People will understand.
- Remember your audience is on your side. Your listeners want you to do well because they will feel more relaxed if you exude an exterior calm.
- Keep a sense of perspective. This is not a life and death scenario and probably as speaker you will be feeling the importance of the event more than your audience does.
- Muster up the courage to have a go – remember this is where true confidence lies.
- Get feedback. Build experience and ideas for your next presentation.

Being assertive when writing

Whether you are writing a lengthy report or a short email exchange, it is important to achieve the appropriate tone and style for your reader, your document and your organisation. Assertiveness means being clear and transparent, so that your reader receives the right message.

Of course, body language and tone of voice (see page 25) are lost in written communication, so getting the mix of tone and message right for your reader is important. People often say they are offended by the tone of a message or email because it is seen as blunt or abrupt. Equally, if you are overly polite, obsequious or over friendly (especially if it is someone you do not know well or have never met), this can be off-putting.

If you are writing a fundraising bid, you need to be able to assert the strength of your bid and the project itself as well as your organisation's capability to deliver it. Remaining assertive when writing bids allows you to showcase your abilities.

- Spend more time planning and preparing to write than writing itself.
- Allow enough time to plan, write and edit your work – diarise it.
- Retain clarity of your purpose ('Why am I writing this? What outcome do I want?'), your readers ('Who are they? What are their expectations?') and your content ('What exactly do I want to say? How will I structure it?').
- Get the tone and style right for your audience and purpose. For example, if you are writing a fundraising bid, make sure your language is assertive in a positive way: say 'we will' rather than 'we can try' or 'we aim to ensure'.
- Always be as concise as you can and keep paragraphs short with one topic per paragraph.
- Use bullet points where you can summarise your message in a direct way. This makes your content punchier and more assertive.
- When writing emails, choose your words carefully to suit your reader. Some people exchange pleasantries before getting down to business, while others

prefer to go straight in. If you know the person, you can reflect their style, and if you do not, go for a middle road – friendly but professional approach.
- Define your goal. For example, if you are making a request, put your ask upfront to show confidence by putting your 'bottom line' at the top.
- Finally, check your tone for anger or accusation with a trusted friend. What might sound neutral to you when writing may come across as condescending or aggressive without a face and tone of voice. Check for understanding on first reading and edit out any unnecessary words or ambiguities.

Handling feedback

Being able to handle feedback is essential to ensure you come across as assertive rather than passive or aggressive and, ultimately, leads to greater confidence. Feedback – sometimes outright criticism – may not always be objectively true but may hold some truth for the person delivering it. There are two ways your confidence can take a knock when it comes to handling feedback: the first is you feel anxious about the 'accusation' and tend to over-apologise; the second is you deny the 'accusation' through defensiveness, resulting in conflict and more bad feelings. When dealing with feedback:

> **Top tip**
> Remember: you always have a choice not to accept criticism, but some of the toughest feedback – although hard to take at the time – can be what helps you grow in confidence most.

- Listen with empathy and an open mind.
- Seek specific information. Do not just accept vague generalities.
- Notice the impact you have on others and the situation in question.
- Try not to be defensive, interrupt or justify.
- If the feedback is valid, acknowledge it.
- Feedback can be hard to give, so say thanks.
- Act on the feedback if you believe it will make a difference, but do not feel you have to respond straight away.

Chapter 4

Looking the part

This chapter is about creating a confident first impression and demonstrating credibility.

Looking and sounding confident

There is often a gap between how we see ourselves and the way others see us. People make judgements about us, just as we do about them, which may be misplaced and ill-judged at times. Managing your awareness of yourself and others is part of developing your emotional intelligence and also helps you to present yourself both professionally and confidently.

We create impressions through our non-verbal behaviour (appearance, body language and demeanour) and verbal cues (pitch, tone, volume and so on). When you present yourself in a manner that is both true to yourself and valued by others, you create positive impressions that enhance self-confidence, build good relationships and improve performance.

An appropriate professional image is essential to any successful career, no matter your age or field. Remember that first impressions are critical: the consensus of psychological studies suggests that people form their first impression within a matter of seconds after meeting you. Whether you are looking for a job, are starting a new one or are a long-term employee at an organisation, it is helpful to review the elements of creating a positive image.

Dress for success

You need to know the dress code appropriate for your place of work. Every organisation is different and may have written guidelines on what is expected. Dressing for the context you are working in, bearing in mind the aims of your organisation and the people you serve, is also important. Consider what your clothes and appearance say about you and your relationship with your organisation and those you meet in the course of your work. For example, while you might wear a suit when meeting a funder, a pair of jeans and a t-shirt might be more appropriate in informal outreach settings. Misjudging the dress code can affect how you are perceived and how people behave towards you, and ultimately it can undermine your confidence. Once you understand what dress code is expected in the context of your work, you can apply your own style choices to help you feel more comfortable and truer to yourself. Your professional attire should say 'I belong here' and help you feel that way too.

Body language and the verbal message

Human beings use a wide variety of communication styles. They may have similarities, but – like their signature – each person's style is unique (which of course makes life more interesting!). Research in 1967 largely led by Professor Albert Mehrabian at the University of California suggested that when we communicate face to face, less than 10% of the meaning and impact comes from the words we say. The remaining 90% is determined by our non-verbal communication:

> **Where next?**
> Watch Amy Cuddy's TED talk on body language and confidence:
>
> www.ted.com/talks/amy_cuddy_your_body_langua ge_may_shape_who_you _are?

facial expressions, eye contact, gestures, body posture, spatial distance, general appearance and tone of voice. These factors greatly impact our message.

Significantly, Professor Mehrabian's research found that over a third of communication impact comes from the tone of voice. Think of a short phrase or even a single word like 'yes' and consider the different shades of meaning conveyed by the way you say it. Sometimes, tone of voice impedes interactions with others and undermines confidence.

The language you use matters too. Know your audience and use language they will understand – do not use unfamiliar jargon. Decide what you are going to say in advance and own your messages using 'I' language. Make your tone of voice and body language match your words: do not say one thing but mean another. Taking ownership and responsibility for the ideas you express demonstrates confidence.

If you want to look and sound confident, and for your message to be received accurately and as intended, you need to be aware of your body language. Noting your visual and vocal behaviour will help you to choose behaviours that will convey the right message. The table below illustrates which assertive behaviours can help you show your confidence through body language and, conversely, what behaviours you should avoid.

	Confident and assertive body language	Unconfident and unassertive body language
Face	Relaxed, smiling and saying hello to people.	Too serious, frowning, smiling with your mouth only or eyebrows raised in disbelief.
Eye contact	Looking people in the eye when speaking and listening.	Staring or fixing your eyes uncomfortably on someone, or looking down and avoiding eye contact.

Body movement	Sitting and standing up straight, offering a firm handshake and using open body language (such as facing the person speaking and squaring your body towards others without folded arms).	Slouching and hunching shoulders, hand wringing or fiddling with objects, stepping back from others, covering your mouth with your hand when speaking, or any nervous movements with legs and feet.
Voice	Not too loud or too quiet, steady and firm, tone is middle range and warm.	Too quiet or too loud (shouting), monotone without much expression, or using sarcastic or whining tone.
Speaking pattern	Fluent and with natural pauses, emphasising key words without too much repetition, steady and with even pace.	Hesitant and with too many pauses, frequent throat clearing or abrupt clipped phrases.

Building credibility

Credibility can be defined as the quality of being trusted and believed in. When you know others have faith in you, your confidence grows as does your influence.

- **Be on time.** Punctuality when attending meetings, appointments and other events can convey a strong sense of professionalism, as it shows respect for your colleagues and their responsibilities.
- **Be prepared.** By preparing and organising your materials beforehand, you can avoid coming across as nervous or uninformed. Take the time to do the necessary reading or research and ensure you have read the agenda and papers before a meeting. This way, you will appear calm and confident – not ruffling and shuffling papers at the last minute.

- **Be organised.** Pay attention to your time management. Take time out to plan and prepare – block out time in your diary to do this. Allot time for dealing with emails rather than allowing yourself to be constantly distracted. You can set timers to better understand how long each task takes and see how you might optimise your time.

- **Be accountable.** Take responsibility for your actions even when this may be uncomfortable. Be clear about the key accountabilities and boundaries of your job role and what is expected from you. Do not be afraid to quickly admit and own your mistakes. People have more confidence in you when you are able to recognise your errors yourself.

- **Be ready to learn and step up to new opportunities.** By showing an interest in developing yourself and benefiting your organisation you signal that you are prepared to take on new things. Try volunteering for internal projects, offering to help a colleague (even if you are not sure about the work involved) or learning a new skill.

- **Be prepared to ask for help and raise questions.** Ask for clarification or admit you need some help instead of pretending to know something when you really do not. You will not damage your credibility by asking, especially when showing your motivation to better understand your job. Asking questions demonstrates honesty and integrity.

- **Be positive.** It can be hard to remain positive when things are not going well, but if you can find the silver lining even in the most difficult situations, you will show a confident persona. When faced with unfamiliar or challenging situations, do you tend to give up without even trying? Consider approaching such situations with an open mindset. Think about what you *can* do and how you can contribute.

Chapter 5

If things go wrong

This chapter is about picking yourself up when things go wrong and looking after your well-being.

Everyone fails and has things go wrong, and learning how to thrive, in spite of your most epic mistakes, takes practice. When something does not work out, confidence can take a real knock-back and you beat yourself up. This self-blame can inhibit you from taking future risks and make you miss out on opportunities, because the mindset is that you are going to fail. Remember: you are more than your failures or mistakes. With new challenges, ask yourself 'What is the worst that could happen?' Things may not work out the way you want, but something good may still come out of it. There are always things to help you bounce back and pick yourself up when things go wrong.

- **Take a break.** When things go wrong, it is easy for your negative inner voice to enter a gloomy spiral where you feel there is no way forward. Remember, when you are in 'fight or flight' mode, your rational-thinking brain virtually shuts down. Taking time out helps you regain composure. Once calmer, you will be able to think through the situation in a more measured way.
- **Understand your emotions.** Do not deny your feelings when things go wrong and be careful not to catastrophise what has happened.
- **Think about your goals.** When calmer, you will be able to think about your longer-term goals. You will be able to see more clearly and summon the courage to resume the path towards your objectives.

- **Remind yourself of past successes.** Just a few mistakes can overshadow the many successes in your life. It is easy to take for granted small achievements that may have made a big difference to your growth and development.
- **Remember you are not alone.** You are not the first or only person to fail at something or make a mistake. Talk to any friends and colleagues and they may share stories of their own bloomers.
- **Practise self-compassion.** Who really is being hard on us when things go wrong? It is usually ourselves! If you imagine it was your best friend in such a situation, what would you say to them?

Developing resilience

By dealing with your setbacks, you are building your resilience. Resilience is the ability to bounce back when things do not go as planned and is strongly linked to self-confidence. Resilient people are confident they are going to succeed eventually, despite the failures or stresses they might be facing. This belief enables you to take more risks and develop confidence and a strong sense of self. Develop your resilience in the following ways:

> **Where next?**
>
> Find out how resilient you are and how to bounce back by completing this questionnaire:
>
> www.mindtools.com/pages/article/resilience-quiz.htm

- Learn to be flexible. Resilient people understand that things change and carefully made plans will often crumble. As Mike Tyson, the famous boxer, reportedly said before a fight, 'Everyone's got a plan until they get a punch in the face!'
- Set yourself some goals. Working towards an aim will give you a sense of purpose, making you feel more grounded and confident.
- Learn to relax. Find ways of taking time out from work stresses to look after yourself. Just working harder does not make you more confident or successful. Learn from your mistakes and failures. Practise viewing hiccups as learning opportunities.

- Work on your emotional intelligence, especially self-management. Understand your own feelings and emotions and you will better understand others.

Your well-being is important

Looking after yourself is an important part of building your self-confidence, and yet it is so easy to put it on the backburner with competing work and life demands. A good work–life balance, knowing your personal goals and understanding your stress triggers (such as public speaking or taking on new responsibilities) all help when things feel out of control and your confidence takes a dip.

Work–life balance

A healthy work–life balance means different things to us all. It might be:

- Meeting deadlines at work while still having time for friends and family.
- Having time to lead a healthy life with regular sleeping and eating patterns.
- Being able to switch off outside work time.
- Having time to pursue interests and hobbies outside work.

Maintaining this balance can be challenging if you have other demanding roles outside work, such as caring responsibilities. We can easily slip into bad habits and normalise working long hours or being under extreme stress, especially if colleagues are doing the same and the culture we work in encourages this. Look honestly at your current work–life balance:

- **Pause and pay attention to your feelings.** What is currently causing you stress and how is it affecting your work and personal life? Understanding your feelings can help you decide what changes you want to make.
- **Re-prioritise.** Evaluate what needs to change and consider your alternatives. Do you have flexibility around working hours? Can you work from home some days of the week?

Improving your well-being

Committing to just one or two small changes a week or even month can make a huge difference to your overall well-being. When we see and feel improvements, our confidence also takes a boost. Make sure to:

- **Connect with people** to support your mental well-being. Make time for friends and family.
- **Be physically active**, especially if sitting at the computer all day. This is different for everyone from following a gym programme, to participating in team sports or group activities to going for walks more regularly.
- **Learn new skills.** Practising a new skill may help boost confidence, self-esteem and mental well-being. It could be something simple like trying out a new recipe or an ambitious project at work or learning a new language.
- **Helping others.** Lending a hand to someone who needs your support, volunteering in your community or a simple act of kindness to a stranger – all can really support your mental well-being.
- **Be present.** Try practising mindfulness to improve health physically and mentally. Meditation and yoga will get you started.
- **Connect with nature.** Getting out into the countryside or visiting your local park can greatly improve your mental health.

Where next?
Listen to the BBC's 'Just One Thing' podcasts with Dr Michael Mosley:

www.bbc.co.uk/sounds/brand/p09by3yy

Final word

The confidence journey continues throughout life. We all have the innate ability to master new situations and that is a core aspect of confidence-building. The more you can discover about yourself, your strengths and aspirations, and the more you can bring the real you to work and pursue your goals with energy and commitment, the more confident you will be. And remember: confidence comes not from always being right but from not fearing to be wrong.